T0268814

RUN,
SHEPHERDS,
RUN

RUN, SHEPHERDS, RUN

Poems *for* Advent *and* Christmas

selected and presented by

L. WILLIAM COUNTRYMAN

morehouse

HARRISBURG • LONDON

Biblical quotations are taken from the Authorized
   (or King James) Version.

Morehouse Publishing, P.O. Box 1321, Harrisburg, PA 17105
Morehouse Publishing, The Tower Building, 11 York Road,
   London SE1 7NX
Morehouse Publishing is a Continuum imprint.

Cover art (shepherds) courtesy of The Crosiers

Cover design by Corey Kent

Library of Congress Cataloging-in-Publication Data

   Run, shepherds, run : poems for Advent and Christmas / selected and presented by L. William Countryman.
      p.   cm.
   Includes bibliographical references.
   ISBN 0-8192-2151-1 (pbk.)
   1. Christmas—Poetry. 2. Christian poetry, English. 3. Christian poetry, American. 4. Advent—Poetry. I.Countryman, Louis William, 1941-
PR1195.C49R86   2005
821.008'0334—dc22

                                                          2004025892

Printed in the United States of America

05 06 07 08 09   10 9 8 7 6 5 4 3 2 1

CONTENTS

An Invitation

*I*f you are weary of having Christmas shaped for you
by the pleadings of retail advertising—
Buy this! Buy that!
Do you really have enough stuff yet? . . .

If you have come to dread the hectic pace of
Christmas preparations and the collapse that follows—
Hurry, hurry to make everything perfect for the 25th!
And then, Boom! It's all over . . .

If you find the secular mythology
of the perfect family Christmas—
with all your kin in perfect accord,
and peace reigning not only in the world
but even in the household—
more depressing than encouraging . . .

And if you have a vague sense that
something better is possible,
that Christmas may have something to say
to real people living amid the real struggles
of the world, then:

I invite you to prepare for Christmas
in a different way this Advent.

I invite you to spend time with some short poems
that may help you treat Christmas
not as an exercise in denial but as
an affirmation of hope and joy,
even in the midst of the realities of human life.

I invite you to find here a more rewarding path
toward the celebration of Jesus' birth,
one shaped not by commercial hype or secular myths
but by reflection on the human condition
and a deep hope rooted in the birth of the Child.

Nothing against the gifts and the feasting! These are important parts of the celebration. But they are the means, not the end. The real purpose is to rejoice in God's generosity and the new hope made possible by this birth.

—LWC

Thoughts on
Reading Poetry

Not all of us feel particularly comfortable or at home with poetry. Here are a few suggestions that may make your reading more enjoyable and rewarding:

1. *Read aloud,* if you can. Part of what is wonderful about poetry is the sound. You *can* hear it a little bit inside your head, but it's always better read aloud. And sometimes, oddly enough, the poem reveals its sense more easily when you read it that way.

2. *Read it more than once.* If it's a poem you've never read before, the first reading is often just a matter of figuring out what the words mean and how they're hooked together in sentences. The second reading often gives a much better sense of the poem as a whole.

3. *Accept that you'll relate more easily to some poems than to others.* Nobody likes all poems equally. You'll probably find one day's selection more rewarding than another's. Keep with it! There is a mix of styles and levels of difficulty here. And you never know what will light up unexpectedly for you.

4. *Read with the punctuation more than the line endings.* The sense often runs over from one line to the next. The punctuation is usually your best guide to units of meaning, such as phrases and clauses. The line endings do sometimes make us hesitate just a bit. That's fine. Just don't take them too seriously.

5. *Talk with somebody else about it*, if you have the chance. Often the way another person reads the poem will be a little different, and sometimes that will spark new insights for you.

With the older poems of this collection, I have taken some liberties in modernizing punctuation and spelling. I have left more recent poetry as I found it except that the publisher has chosen to substitute American spellings.

First Week of Advent

"*A*dvent" comes from a Latin word that means "coming" or "arrival," as when some great figure like the emperor arrived during a tour of the provinces. The season of Advent, beginning four Sundays before Christmas, is a focused, reflective time of preparation for our celebration of the humble birth of Jesus at Bethlehem. It also reminds us that we await another coming of Jesus, a coming in majesty at the end of all things. The second coming fulfills the promise of the first. Both together embody our human hope for a world of justice and peace.

We begin, this week, with an old Advent tradition of meditating on the "Four Last Things": Death, Judgment, Hell, and Heaven—all themes associated with the Second Coming. It may seem odd to prepare for Christmas by reflecting on the end of life, but it actually starts us off where we are, in a world of limits and moral ambiguity. It reminds us that we humans are still far from being in a world of enduring peace, justice, and good will.

Then, as we turn our gaze toward the child at Bethlehem, we recognize that this birth is just a beginning. We are still in the midst of understanding it and learning to live in accord with it. Advent allows us to acknowledge the sorrows and incompleteness of human existence in the here and now and so to greet God's new beginning in the manger with greater joy.

Advent Sunday

This well-known Advent hymn strikes the keynote of the season: Christ will return to establish justice on earth, to bind up what is broken, to restore the reign of God among us. Having experienced human poverty, vulnerability, and suffering, Jesus is all the more equipped to bind up the broken heart and cure the bleeding soul.

PHILIP DODDRIDGE

> Hark! the glad sound! the Savior comes,
>   the Savior promised long:
> let every heart prepare a throne,
>   and every voice a song.
>
> He comes, the prisoners to release
>   in Satan's bondage held;
> the gates of brass before him burst,
>   the iron fetters yield.
>
> He comes, the broken heart to bind,
>   the bleeding soul to cure;
> and with the treasures of his grace
>   to enrich the humble poor.
>
> Our glad hosannas, Prince of Peace,
>   thy welcome shall proclaim;
> and heaven's eternal arches ring
>   with thy beloved Name.

Drawn from The Hymnal 1982, hymn 71.

Monday of the First Week
of Advent: Death

John Donne was a great preacher and poet, one of whose hall-marks is passionate intensity. Today and tomorrow, we have two of his "Holy Sonnets." Today's announces the end of death's terrors.

Benjamin Britten wrote great musical settings of this and the following poem in his "Holy Sonnets of John Donne."

Holy Sonnet X

JOHN DONNE

> Death be not proud, though some have callèd thee
> Mighty and dreadful, for thou art not so,
> For those whom thou think'st thou dost overthrow
> Die not, poor death, nor yet canst thou kill me.
> From rest and sleep, which but thy pictures be,
> Much pleasure—then from thee much more must flow;
> And soonest our best men with thee do go,
> Rest of their bones, and soul's delivery.
> Thou art slave to fate, chance, kings, and desperate men,
> And dost with poison, war, and sickness dwell,
> And poppy or charms can make us sleep as well
> And better than thy stroke. Why swell'st thou then?
> One short sleep past, we wake eternally,
> And death shall be no more. Death, thou shalt die.

Drawn from *The Complete Poetry and Selected Prose of John Donne*, edited by Charles M. Coffin (New York: The Modern Library, 1952), 250–51.

Tuesday of the First Week of Advent: Judgment

Here, Donne calls on angelic trumpets to summon all of humanity, living and dead, for judgment. But then he reverses himself and says, "Wait! I need time for repentance." At the end, he suggests, with a touch of irony, that he needs not only the divine gift of God's own life but also the grace of a repentant heart to reassure him that God truly intends his good.

Much of the poem's imagery, including the angelic trumpet, is drawn from Paul's description of the Second Coming in 1 Thessalonians 4:13–18.

Holy Sonnet VII

JOHN DONNE

> At the round earth's imagin'd corners, blow
> Your trumpets, Angels, and arise, arise
> From death, you numberless infinities
> Of souls, and to your scatter'd bodies go—
> All whom the flood did and fire shall o'erthrow,
> All whom war, dearth, age, agues, tyrannies,
> Despair, law, chance hath slain, and you whose eyes,
> Shall behold God, and never taste death's woe.[1]
>
> But let them sleep, Lord, and me mourn a space,
> For if, above all these, my sins abound,
> 'Tis late to ask abundance of thy grace
> When we are there; here on this lowly ground,
> Teach me how to repent; for that's as good
> As if thou hadst seal'd my pardon with thy blood.

---

1. "you whose eyes . . . woe"—those still alive at the Second Coming.

6

Drawn from *The Complete Poetry and Selected Prose of John Donne*, edited by Charles M. Coffin (New York: The Modern Library, 1952), 249.

Wednesday of the First Week of Advent: Hell

Hell and Heaven are metaphors for our deepest human fears and hopes—the danger and the promise that we discern in ourselves, as individuals and as groups. This is not to say that they are unreal, but that language uses them as images to gesture toward things within ourselves that are deep and hard to speak of.

In the world of the last century and more, hell has most often taken the face of human violence: war, conquest, pogrom, totalitarianism, genocide, terrorism. The worst part of it is that it often masquerades as something high-minded. Bruce Dawe, in this poem, captures something of the way in which revolutionary hopes for good can be transformed into hell on earth. The last line suggests that the process will repeat itself. One of our Advent hopes is that God can introduce a new kind of salvation that is not merely a step toward some new hell.

only the beards are different
BRUCE DAWE

Among the first to go are always a few
Of the strong man's friends, crumpling up
Against the sun-pocked wall, relieved at last
Of the terrible burden of his friendship.
Cruel necessity follows him everywhere.
And the face that was once a dream
Of a patch of baked earth to the landless
And a living wage has lost its inner light,
Faded, and now, deathless and untrue
Flaps in the memory like a wind-blown poster.
Behind the monolithic smile, the frighteningly
Public eyes, a thousand trigger-fingers tense;

Sadist and pimp resume
Their tricky trades. Caught in two minds,
Men look the other way when truth cries out, that leprous
Mendicant whose importunity must be discouraged.
Travelers find the once-welcoming
Doors closed to them now; over the evening meal
The children are eyed suspiciously, radios
Turned up louder and louder to cover
All the embarrassing noises a revolution makes
In passing—the tumbrils,[1] the firing-squads, the screams
From the underground prison,
The rifle-butts at the door, the conspirators' whisper,
The drums, the marching-songs, the hysterical spiel
Of bandaleroed barkers plugging the ancient wares . . .

Somewhere the country's savior cries in his sleep.

Drawn from Bruce Dawe, *Condolences of the Season: Selected Poems* (Melbourne: Longman Cheshire, 1971), 2.

---

1. "Tumbrils": Two-wheeled farm carts of a type used to carry prisoners to the guillotine in the French Revolution.

Thursday of the First Week of Advent: Heaven

Our awareness of the terrible evil in the human self, something that has become repeatedly evident in the past hundred years, means that we sometimes look to the world of nature as a more adequate sign of what the universe could be, ourselves included. In this poem, Emily Dickinson turns to the natural world and its moments of particular splendor in just such a way, then wonders how humanity can ever find a place in that picture.

Dickinson's punctuation is idiosyncratic. But you will find that the dashes are good indicators for pauses in reading the lines aloud.

EMILY DICKINSON

> "Heaven" has different Signs—to me—
> Sometimes, I think that Noon
> Is but a symbol of the Place—
> And when again, at Dawn,
>
> A mighty look runs round the World
> And settles in the Hills—
> An Awe if it should be like that
> Upon the Ignorance steals—
>
> The Orchard, when the Sun is on—
> The Triumph of the Birds
> When they together Victory make—
> Some Carnivals of Clouds—
>
> The Rapture of a finished Day—
> Returning to the West—
> All these—remind us of the place
> That Men call "Paradise"—

Itself be fairer—we suppose—
But how Ourself, shall be
Adorned, for a Superior Grace—
Not yet, our eyes can see—[1]

Drawn from *The Complete Poems of Emily Dickinson*, edited by Thomas H. Johnson (Boston: Little, Brown, n.d.), 280–81.

---

1. Cf. 1 John 3:2: "It doth not yet appear what we shall be; but we know that, when he shall appear, we shall be like him."

Friday of the First Week of Advent: Infancy

This poem is not about the baby Jesus in particular, but about infancy as such. Henry Vaughan saw an integrity and innocence in early childhood that contrasted sharply with adult life. This infant quality of new beginning and of closeness to the Holy is part of what we see in the story of Jesus' birth and part of what makes it powerful for us.

The Retreat

HENRY VAUGHAN

> Happy those early days! when I
> Shined in my Angel-infancy.
> Before I understood this place
> Appointed for my second race,[1]
> Or taught my soul to fancy aught
> But a white, celestial thought,
> When yet I had not walked, above
> A mile, or two, from my first love[2]
> And looking back (at that short space)
> Could see a glimpse of his bright face;
> When on some gilded cloud, or flower
> My gazing soul would dwell an hour,
> And in those weaker glories spy
> Some shadows of eternity;
> Before I taught my tongue to wound
> My conscience with a sinful sound,

---

1. "second race"—earthly human life

2. "first love"—God

Or had the black art to dispense
A several sin to every sense,
But felt through all this fleshly dress
Bright shoots of everlastingness.
　　O how I long to travel back
And tread again that ancient track!
That I might once more reach that plain,
Where first I left my glorious train,
From whence the enlightened spirit sees
That shady city of palm trees;[3]
But (ah!) my soul with too much stay
Is drunk, and staggers in the way.
Some men a forward motion love,
But I by backward steps would move,
And when this dust falls to the urn[4]
In that state I came return.

Drawn from *Henry Vaughan: The Complete Poems*, edited by Alan Rudrum
(New Haven: Yale University Press, 1981), 172–73.

---

3. In the Bible, the city of palm trees is Jericho (Deuteronomy 34:3); but
Vaughan seems to be thinking of the New Jerusalem, which John described as
shaded by the Trees of Life (Revelation 22:1–5).

4. "the urn"—the grave

Saturday of the First Week of Advent: Mary

One great theme of Advent is the celebration of Mary, the Mother of Jesus, and the generous faith with which she responded to the angel's announcement that she would bear a child. Her willingness to undertake this risk, even including the sorrows that she may have foreseen, is an example of all the best that graced humanity is capable of.

The Knot

HENRY VAUGHAN

> Bright Queen of Heaven! God's Virgin Spouse
>> The glad world's blessed maid!
> Whose beauty tied life to thy house,
>> And brought us saving aid.
>
> Thou art the true loves-knot; by thee
>> God is made our ally,
> And man's inferior essence he
>> With his did dignify.[1]
>
> For coalescent by that band
>> We are his body grown,
> Nourished with favors from his hand
>> Whom for our head we own[2]

---

1. In the Incarnation, Jesus is truly human and truly God, "dignifying" human nature with the divine.

2. "own"—acknowledge. Jesus is head of creation and of the church (Colossians 1:15-20).

And such a knot, what arm dares loose,
  What life, what death can sever?
Which us in him, and him in us
  United keeps for ever.

Drawn from *Henry Vaughan: The Complete Poems*, edited by Alan Rudrum
(New Haven: Yale University Press, 1981), 272.

Second Week of Advent

*T*his week, we will revisit some of the "Four Last Things," and we also turn our gaze a little more onto Jesus' birth at Bethlehem. Christians have long spoken of John the Baptist as Jesus' "Forerunner," preparing the way for his life and ministry. Luke tells us that he was also Jesus' cousin. The drama involves more than just the central characters of Mary and Jesus.

This will be a good week, too, to take a look at the subject of gifts, for December 6, which always falls in the first or second week of Advent, is the feast of St. Nicholas of Myra. A fourth-century bishop, he is the older, less secularized version of Santa Claus, revered for his generosity to the poor and his protection of children.

Second Sunday
of Advent

In this poem, Christina Rossetti focuses particularly on Advent as a time of longing for reunion, in the age to come, with our beloved family and friends who have died and are with Jesus. She borrows extensively from biblical texts: the figure of the Watchman from Isaiah 21, the wise virgins with their lamps from Jesus' parable in Matthew 25, the "holding fast" from Jacob's wrestling with the angel in Genesis 32, and the concluding invitation to love from Song of Solomon 2. The last gives to the whole poem a note of erotic longing and fulfillment typical of much Christian spirituality.

Advent

CHRISTINA ROSSETTI

> This Advent moon shines cold and clear,
>   These Advent nights are long;
> Our lamps have burned year after year
>   And still their flame is strong.
> "Watchman, what of the night?" we cry
>   Heart-sick with hope deferred:
> "No speaking signs are in the sky,"
>   Is still the watchman's word.
>
> The Porter watches at the gate,
>   The servants watch within;
> The watch is long betimes and late,
>   The prize is slow to win.
> "Watchman, what of the night?" but still
>   His answer sounds the same:
> "No daybreak tops the utmost hill,
>   Nor pale our lamps of flame."

One to another hear them speak
    The patient virgins wise:
"Surely He is not far to seek"—
    "All night we watch and rise."
"The days are evil looking back,
    The coming days are dim;
Yet count we not His promise slack,
    But watch and wait for Him."

One with another, soul with soul,
    They kindle fire from fire:
"Friends watch us who have touched the goal."[1]
    "They urge us, come up higher."
"With them shall rest our waysore feet,
    With them is built our home,
With Christ."—"They sweet, but He most sweet,
    Sweeter than honeycomb."

There no more parting, no more pain,
    The distant ones brought near,
The lost so long are found again,
    Long lost but longer dear:
Eye hath not seen, ear hath not heard,
    Nor heart conceived that rest,
With them our good things long deferred,
    With Jesus Christ our Best.

We weep because the night is long,
    We laugh for day shall rise,
We sing a slow contented song
    And knock at Paradise.
Weeping we hold Him fast, Who wept
    For us, we hold Him fast;
And will not let Him go except
    He bless us first or last.

---

1. "touched the goal"—are with Christ in Paradise

Weeping we hold Him fast tonight;
    We will not let Him go
Till daybreak smite our wearied sight
    And summer smite the snow:
Then figs shall bud, and dove with dove
    Shall coo the livelong day;
Then He shall say, "Arise, My love,
    My fair one, come away."

Drawn from *Christina Rossetti: The Complete Poems*, text by R. W. Crump (London: Penguin Books, 2001), 62–64.

Monday of the Second Week of Advent: The Unknown

The Advent summons "Come!" implies that we seek a communion with God and with Christ that we do not yet enjoy. Such a communion is bound to go beyond anything that we can imagine or believe. To know it fully we would already have to be in it.

Elizabeth Smith's hymn reminds us that our Advent expectation is always directed toward what we do not yet truly know. Our believing points us toward the Holy but does not yet fully reveal God.

ELIZABETH J. SMITH

> God in the darkness, God beyond our knowing,
> patient creator, seed in secret growing,
> rock of the living water ever flowing:[1]
> > come and renew us.
>
> God in the darkness, God in all our grieving,
> friend of our tears, companion never leaving,
> drawing us past the limits of believing:
> > come and renew us.
>
> God in the darkness, God of holy dreaming,
> giver of hope, and pledge of our redeeming,
> Spirit of truth, our memory and meaning;
> > come and renew us.

Drawn from Elizabeth J. Smith, *Praise the God of Grace: Hymns for Inclusive Worship* (Mt Waverley, Victoria: St Stephen's Anglican Church, 1990), Hymn 5.

---

1. The image refers to the rock from which God commanded Moses to bring forth "living" (i.e. flowing) water, Exodus 17.

Tuesday of the Second Week
of Advent: Hell

Our experience of hell is not only social and public, as in last
Wednesday's poem by Bruce Dawe, but also private and inter-
nal. We may experience it as an interior doubt, distress, or self-
loathing that, as Gerard Manley Hopkins says here, can only
be that of "the lost." There is little sign of relief in this poem.
The poet is trapped. And, indeed, that is how our experience
of hell always feels until it is interrupted by some unexpected
gift of grace.

GERARD MANLEY HOPKINS

> I wake and feel the fell[1] of dark, not day.
> What hours, O what black hoürs we have spent
> This night! what sights you, heart, saw; ways you went!
> And more must, in yet longer light's delay.
>
> With witness I speak this. But where I say
> Hours I mean years, mean life. And my lament
> Is cries countless, cries like dead letters sent
> To dearest him that lives alas! away.
>
> I am gall, I am heartburn. God's most deep decree
> Bitter would have me taste: my taste was me;
> Bones built in me, flesh filled, blood brimmed the curse.
>
> Selfyeast of spirit a dull dough sours. I see
> The lost are like this, and their scourge to be
> As I am mine, their sweating selves; but worse.

---

1. "fell"—As a noun, "fell" means an animal pelt; here it also has overtones of
its meaning as an adjective ("dire, menacing") and as the past tense of the
verb "fall."

Drawn from *The Poems of Gerard Manley Hopkins*, 4th ed., edited by W. H. Gardner and N. H. MacKenzie (London: Oxford University Press, 1970), 101.

Wednesday of the Second Week of Advent: Heaven

Rossetti echoes Psalm 24, with its refrain of "Lift up your heads, O ye gates!" and its promise that the righteous will ascend the hill of the Lord. In modern English, "the righteous" may sound dull and self-satisfied, rather like "the pious." But in the language of Scripture, the "righteous" are those who do justice, who have already shown themselves to be citizens of the age to come by conducting themselves here and now with faithfulness toward God and respect toward all people. "Keeping the truth" is another way to describe this devotion to justice.

CHRISTINA ROSSETTI

> Hark! the Alleluias of the great salvation
>   Still beginning, never ending, still begin,
> The thunder of an endless adoration:
> Open ye the gates, that the righteous nation
>   Which have kept the truth may enter in.
>
> Roll ye back, ye pearls, on your twelvefold station:[1]
>   No more deaths to die, no more fights to win!
> Lift your heads, ye gates, that the righteous nation
> Led by the Great Captain of their sole salvation,
>   Having kept the truth, may enter in.

Drawn from *Christina Rossetti: The Complete Poems*, text by R. W. Crump (London: Penguin Books, 2001), 454.

---

1. Revelation 21:21 describes the heavenly city, New Jerusalem, as having twelve gates, each made of a single pearl.

Thursday of the Second Week of Advent: John the Baptist

John the Baptist was the kind of prophet who found himself so much at odds with his times that he could only retreat to the wilderness to proclaim his message of repentance. He taught that people have to experience a great change of direction, of perspective, and of meaning before they can become once again friends of God.

John must have been an alarming sight, gaunt from a meager diet and clothed in coarse skins or haircloth (Mark 1:6). William Drummond suggests here that his message did not make much of an impression on his contemporaries—often a problem for prophets. But true prophets have to prophesy anyway.

For the Baptist

WILLIAM DRUMMOND

The last and greatest Herald of Heaven's King,
Girt with rough skins, hies to the deserts wild
Among that savage brood the woods forth bring,
Which he than man more harmless found and mild.[1]
His food was blossoms and what young doth spring—[2]
With honey that from virgin hives distilled;
Parched body, hollow eyes, some uncouth thing
Made him appear, long since from earth exiled.
There burst he forth, "All ye, whose hopes rely
On God, with me amidst these deserts mourn.
Repent, repent, and from old errors turn."

---

1. He found the wild animals easier to live with than humanity.

2. "what young doth spring"—young shoots of plants

Who listened to his voice, obey'd his cry?
  Only the echoes which he made relent
  Rung from their marble caves, "Repent, repent."

Drawn from *The Oxford Book of Seventeenth Century Verse*, chosen by H. J. C. Grierson and G. Bullough (Oxford: Clarendon Press, 1934), 264.

Friday of the Second Week of Advent: Gifts

Giftgiving may have come to dominate Christmas too much, but it isn't just a secular imposition on the feast. Gifts are of the essence of it: above all God's gift of becoming fully human in Mary's womb, but also the gifts others brought to Jesus. The giving and receiving of gifts are a necessary part of any rich human existence.

Nothing is quite clear or certain in this poem by Kevin Hart. Is the mysterious gift from a human lover or from God? Given all the shape-shifting it does, can we even think of it as a definable object? Whatever it is, it transforms the speaker and puts life on a completely different footing. By the end, the speaker can't tell what is gift anymore and what is not. Life has become gift, gift life.

The Gift

KEVIN HART

> One day the gift arrives—outside your door,
> Left on a windowsill, inside the mailbox,
> Or in the hallway, far too large to lift.
>
> Your postman shrugs his shoulders, the police
> Consult a statute, and the cat miaows.
> No name, no signature, and no address,
>
> Only, "To you, my dearest one, my all . . ."
> One day it fits snugly in your pocket,
> Then fills the backyard like afternoon in Spring.
>
> Monday morning, and it's there at work—
> Already ahead of you, or left behind
> Amongst the papers, files and photographs;

And were there lipstick smudges down the side
Or have they just appeared? What a headache!
And worse, people have begun to talk:

"You lucky thing!" they say, or roll their eyes.
Nights find you combing the directory
(A glass of straw-colored wine upon the desk)

Still hoping to chance on a forgotten name.
Yet mornings see you happier than before—
After all, the gift has set you up for life.

Impossible to tell, now, what was given
And what was not: slivers of rain on the window,
Those gold-tooled *Oeuvres* of Diderot on the shelf,

The strawberry dreaming in a champagne flute—
Were they part of the gift or something else?
Or is the gift still coming, on its way?

Drawn from Kevin Hart, *New and Selected Poems* (Sydney: Angus & Robertson, 1995), 150–51.

Saturday of the Second Week of Advent: Mary and the Baby

Since we know the rest of the story, we cannot look at the mother and child in Bethlehem without some premonition of what lies ahead—the suffering, the Crucifixion. At the same time, it would be wrong to shortchange the beauty and truth of this moment. R. S. Thomas captures just the breath of it here. It sounds at first like a classic "Madonna and Child" painting, but we catch just a few shadows cast by leafy limbs, suggesting but not quite literally representing what Christians have long called "the tree of the cross."

Mother and Child

R. S. THOMAS

> No clouds overhead;
> no troubles freckling
> the maid's eye. The shadows
> are immediate and are thrown
>
> by upholstered branches,
> not by that angled
> event[1] that from beyond
> the horizon puts its roots
>
> down. This is Eden
> over again. The child
> holds out both his hands
> for the breast's apple. The snake is asleep.

Drawn from R. S. Thomas, *Collected Poems 1945–1990* (London: Phoenix Giant, 1993), 461.

---

1. "angled event"—the Crucifixion

Third Week of Advent

As Christmas Day draws nearer, we celebrate the Incarnation as a moment of sweeping change in the relation of God and humanity. God draws near in the Infant of Bethlehem and dares to take on a real human existence. God will experience weakness and humility, even suffering and death, in order truly to be one of us. We magnify this wonderful, daring, paradoxical undertaking both by speaking of the greatness God set aside and also by recognizing the human vulnerability God now shares with us. It is a time not without its dangers. But it is also a time of new hope.

Third Sunday
of Advent

In Luke's account of the birth of Jesus, we read that Mary went to visit her cousin Elizabeth, mother of John the Baptist. There she praised God with the hymn called "Magnificat," and Christians have long used it as part of evening worship (Luke 1:46–55).

As the days drew near to Christmas, the Latin liturgy of the Middle Ages used a series of special antiphons, or refrains, with the singing of the Magnificat. They began on December 16th or 17th with "O Sapientia" ("O Wisdom"). Today, the refrains are still familiar to us in the form of the Advent hymn "Oh come, oh come, Immanuel." The hymn appeals for peace and unity for all humanity, both God's chosen people Israel and also the rest of us, the "nations" or "Gentiles."

Each salutation is an image drawn from the Scriptures and applied by Christians to Jesus: Wisdom (Proverbs 8 and 9), Lord (Exodus 19:16–25), Branch of Jesse (Isaiah 11), Key of David (Isaiah 22:22), Dayspring (Isaiah 60:1–2), Desire of the Nations/Gentiles (Haggai 2:7; see the older English translations), Emmanuel (Isaiah 7:10–17).

ANONYMOUS

O come, thou Wisdom from on high,
    who orderest all things mightily;
to us the path of knowledge show,
    and teach us in her ways to go.

O come, O come, thou Lord of might,
    who to thy tribes on Sinai's height
in ancient times didst give the law,
    in cloud, and majesty, and awe.

O come, thou Branch of Jesse's tree,[1]
   free them from Satan's tyranny
that trust thy mighty power to save,
   and give them victory o'er the grave.

O come, thou Key of David, come,
   and open wide our heavenly home;
make safe the way that leads on high,
   and close the path to misery.

O come, thou Dayspring[2] from on high,
   and cheer us by thy drawing nigh;
disperse the gloomy clouds of night,
   and death's dark shadow put to flight.

O come, Desire of nations,[3] bind
   in one the hearts of all mankind;
bid thou our sad divisions cease,
   and be thyself our King of Peace.

O come, O come, Emmanuel,[4]
   and ransom captive Israel,
that mourns in lonely exile here
   until the Son of God appear.

Drawn from The Hymnal 1982, hymn 56.

---

1. Jesse was the father of David; Jesus was a descendant of both of them.

2. "Dayspring"—dawn.

3. The "nations," in scriptural language, means the Gentiles.

4. "Emmanuel"—God with us.

Monday of the Third Week
of Advent: Death and Heaven

Henry Vaughan's poetry is often marked by mourning for departed loved ones—a reality that affects many of us at Christmastime. In this poem, he reasserts his confidence that they have simply gone ahead of us and that our own deaths will reunite us with them. He longs for the time when he will no longer merely be peering after them from afar. Having once joined them, he will no longer need a "glass" (telescope) to catch sight of them.

"They are all gone into the world of light!"
HENRY VAUGHAN

They are all gone into the world of light!
    And I alone sit ling'ring here;
Their very memory is fair and bright,
    And my sad thoughts doth clear.

It glows and glitters in my cloudy breast
    Like stars upon some gloomy grove,
Or those faint beams in which this hill is dressed,
    After the sun's remove.[1]

I see them walking in an air of glory,
    Whose light doth trample on my days:
My days, which are at best but dull and hoary,
    Mere glimmering and decays.

O holy hope! and high humility,
    High as the Heavens above!
These are your walks, and you have showed them me
    To kindle my cold love.

---

1. "After the sun's remove"—after sunset

Dear, beauteous death! the jewel of the just,
  Shining nowhere, but in the dark,
What mysteries do lie beyond thy dust,
    Could man outlook that mark!

He that hath found some fledged bird's nest, may know
  At first sight, if the bird be flown;
But what fair well or grove he sings in now,
    That is to him unknown.

And yet, as Angels in some brighter dreams
  Call to the soul when man doth sleep,
So some strange thoughts transcend our wonted themes
    And into glory peep.

If a star were confined into a tomb
  Her captive flames must needs burn there;
But when the hand that locked her up gives room,
    She'll shine through all the sphere.

O Father of eternal life and all
  Created glories under thee!
Resume thy spirit[2] from this world of thrall
    Into true liberty.

Either disperse these mists, which blot and fill
  My perspective (still) as they pass,
Or else remove me hence unto that hill,
    Where I shall need no glass.[3]

Drawn from *Henry Vaughan: The Complete Poems*, edited by Alan Rudrum
(New Haven: Yale University Press, 1981), 246–47.

---

2. "thy spirit"—refers to the poet as a spirit belonging to God rather than to
the Holy Spirit

3. "glass"—telescope

Tuesday of the Third Week
of Advent: Judgment and Grace

Robert Herrick asks here for a loving rather than judging visit
from God. The true purpose of God's judgment, after all, is
rejoicing, not despair.

An "epithalamy," such as Herrick offers God here, is a poem
written to celebrate a wedding. He draws on the ancient tradi-
tion, rooted in the Song of Solomon, of seeing human *eros* as
an essential image of God's love for human beings.

To God

ROBERT HERRICK

> Come to me God; but do not come
> To me, as to the gen'ral Doom,[1]
> In power—nor come thou in that state
> When thou thy Laws didst promulgate,
> Whenas the mountain[2] quak'd for dread,
> And sullen clouds bound up its head.
> No, lay thy stately terrors by
> To talk with me familiarly;
> For if thy thunder-claps I hear,
> I shall less swoon than die for fear.
> Speak thou of love and I'll reply
> By way of epithalamy,
> Or sing of mercy, and I'll suit
> To it my viol and my lute:
> Thus let thy lips but love distill,
> Then come my God, and hap what will.

---

1. "the gen'ral Doom"—the last judgment

2. "the mountain"—Mount Sinai

36

Drawn from *The Poetical Works of Robert Herrick*, edited by F. W. Moorman (London: Oxford University Press, 1921), 383.

Wednesday of the Third Week of Advent: Hell

Not every deity entering into some new incarnation in the world is necessarily beneficent. In Yeats's poem, it is the sphinx, cruel and inscrutable monster of Greek myth, that seeks incarnation into our world, aroused by its very hostility toward the Infant of Bethlehem and toward all of human life. Yeats's poem has proven to be a terrible prelude to much of recent human history.

The Second Coming
WILLIAM BUTLER YEATS

> Turning and turning in the widening gyre
> The falcon cannot hear the falconer;
> Things fall apart; the center cannot hold;
> Mere anarchy is loosed upon the world,
> The blood-dimmed tide is loosed, and everywhere
> The ceremony of innocence is drowned;
> The best lack all conviction, while the worst
> Are full of passionate intensity.
>
> Surely some revelation is at hand;
> Surely the Second Coming is at hand.
> The Second Coming! Hardly are those words out
> When a vast image out of *Spiritus Mundi*[1]
> Troubles my sight: somewhere in sands of the desert
> A shape with lion body and the head of a man,
> A gaze blank and pitiless as the sun,
> Is moving its slow thighs, while all about it
> Reel shadows of the indignant desert birds.

---

1. "*Spiritus Mundi*"—literally, "Spirit of the World"; Yeats's term for the depths of the human imagination, from which archetypal symbols emerge.

The darkness drops again; but now I know
That twenty centuries of stony sleep
Were vexed to nightmare by a rocking cradle,
And what rough beast, its hour come round at last,
Slouches towards Bethlehem to be born?

Drawn from William Butler Yeats, *Selected Poems and Four Plays*, 4th ed. (New York: Scribner, 1996), 89–90.

Thursday of the Third Week of Advent: Incarnation and Salvation

This free-verse Latin poem was written to be sung with the "Alleluia" before the reading of the Gospel at the Eucharist. It presents the ministry of Jesus as a whole, the first and second Advents combining in God's great project of redeeming the world.

Sequence for the First Sunday in Advent
ANONYMOUS, C. 900

> Eternal Health,
> unfailing Life of the world,
> everlasting Light,
> and truly our Redemption,
>
> For grief that the ages
> of humankind should perish
> by the work of the tempter's agents,
>
> Without leaving the heights of heaven,
> you have entered the depths of the world
> with your clemency.
>
> Then by your own free grace
> taking on all that is human,
>
> You have rescued all
> the earthly things
> that had been lost,
> bringing joy to the world.
>
> Our souls and bodies,
> Christ, restore to God
> that you may have us as your
> light-filled dwelling places.

By your first advent, claim us as just and faithful;
by your second, liberate us.

So that when you judge
all deeds
in the bright light,
we, clothed
in unblemished garments,
may follow
your footsteps then
wherever we find them.

Latin text from *The Oxford Book of Medieval Latin Verse*, edited by F. J. E. Raby (Oxford: Clarendon Press, 1959), 133–34, translation by LWC.

Friday of the Third Week of Advent: Grief and Solace

Christmas can be a difficult time for those who are grieving a departed loved one. Alfred Tennyson's poem cycle "In Memoriam" traces several years of his own complex grief for his beloved friend Arthur Henry Hallam. This poem is one of three that speak of the first Christmas after Hallam's death. It evokes the sound of bells from neighboring villages, ringing the complex patterns called "changes." With the shifts in the wind, each village's bells become more or less audible. The poet finds that these sounds associated with the Christmases of his childhood, even though they cannot assuage his grief, still have some power to awaken a memory of joy.

In Memoriam XXVIII

ALFRED TENNYSON

> The time draws near the birth of Christ:
>   The moon is hid; the night is still;
>   The Christmas bells from hill to hill
> Answer each other in the mist.
>
> Four voices of four hamlets round,
>   From far and near, on mead and moor,
>   Swell out and fall, as if a door
> Were shut between me and the sound:
>
> Each voice four changes on the wind,
>   That now dilate, and now decrease,
>   Peace and goodwill, goodwill and peace,
> Peace and goodwill, to all mankind.

This year I slept and woke with pain,
   I almost wish'd no more to wake,
   And that my hold on life would break
Before I heard those bells again:

But they my troubled spirit rule,
   For they controll'd me when a boy;
   They bring me sorrow touch'd with joy,
The merry merry bells of Yule.

Drawn from Alfred Tennyson, *In Memoriam* (Chicago: Henneberry, n.d.), 27–28.

Saturday of the Third Week of Advent: Mary

This late-medieval poem moves from English to Latin and back without missing a beat. I have modernized the English a little and provided translations of the Latin. It celebrates the paradox of the virgin who is a mother and lauds Mary's generosity in cooperating with divine grace to bring the child Jesus into the world. It also looks forward to the life of the age to come when we will be part of Mary's face-to-face community.

Benjamin Britten wrote a beautiful setting of this text, entitled "A Hymn to the Virgin."

Hymn to the Virgin
ANONYMOUS

Of one that is so fair and bright
   velut maris stella,   [like a star of the sea]
brighter than the day is light,
   parens et puella.   [both girl and mother]
I cry to thee; see thou to me!
Lady, pray thy son for me,
   tam pia,   [so faithful!]
that I might come to thee,
   Maria.   [Mary]

All this world was forlorn,
   Eva peccatrice,   [from Eve's sin]
till our Lord was y-born
   de te genetrice.   [from you as his mother]
With *Ave,* there went away   [Hail!]
darkest night and comes the day
   salutis.   [of salvation]

The well springeth out of the
    virtutis.   [virtue]

Lady, Flower of Everything,
    rosa sine spina,   [rose without a thorn]
Thou bore Jesus, Heavenly King,
    gratia divina.   [by divine grace]
Of all maids thou bear'st the prize,
Lady, Queen of Paradise,
    electa.   [chosen one]
Maiden mild, mother *es*
    effecta.   [you've been made (mother)]

I memorized this poem long ago and can't name its source any longer. My apologies to any student of medieval English literature who may find my memory faulty!

Fourth Week of Advent

The final week of Advent varies in length from one day (if Christmas Day falls on a Monday) to seven (if it falls the following Sunday). By this point, we're probably all a little impatient to move from expectation to feast. The user of this little book should skip over to Christmas Eve or Christmas Day as soon as the time comes.

Fourth Sunday
of Advent

The key word of Advent is "Come!" We often think of it purely in terms of Jesus' coming to us, first in the Incarnation, then again at the culmination of the age. In this short poem, Christina Rossetti reminds us that it is also the invitation Jesus extends to us. Indeed, by the end of the poem, it becomes a conversation, in which the longing of both sides is embodied in the same invitation and summons.

Advent

CHRISTINA ROSSETTI

"Come," Thou dost say to Angels,
　　To blessed Spirits, "Come";
"Come," to the Lambs of Thine Own flock,
　　Thy little Ones, "Come home."

"Come"—from the many-mansioned house[1]
　　The gracious word is sent,
"Come"—from the ivory palaces[2]
　　Unto the Penitent.

O Lord, restore us deaf and blind,
　　Unclose our lips tho' dumb;[3]
Then say to us, "I come with speed,"
　　And we will answer, "Come."

Drawn from *Christina Rossetti: The Complete Poems*, text by R. W. Crump (London: Penguin Books, 2001), 731.

---

1. "In my Father's house are many mansions" (John 14:2).

2. Psalm 45:8; Christians have long read this Psalm as a celebration of Jesus as Messiah.

3. "Dumb"—obsolete usage for "without the power of speech."

Monday of the Fourth Week of Advent: The Second Coming

This Greek hymn celebrates Jesus' Second Coming as a moment of perfect beauty as well as justice.

ANONYMOUS

> The King shall come when morning dawns
>   and light triumphant breaks;
> when beauty gilds the eastern hills
>   and life to joy awakes.
>
> Not, as of old, a little child,
>   to bear, and fight, and die,
> but crowned with glory like the sun
>   that lights the morning sky.
>
> The King shall come when morning dawns
>   and earth's dark night is past;
> O haste the rising of that morn,
>   the day that e'er shall last;
>
> and let the endless bliss begin,
>   by weary saints foretold,
> when right shall triumph over wrong,
>   and truth shall be extolled.
>
> The King shall come when morning dawns
>   and light and beauty brings:
> Hail, Christ the Lord! Thy people pray,
>   come quickly, King of kings.

Translation by John Brownlie, as altered in The Hymnal 1982, hymn 73.

Tuesday of the Fourth Week
of Advent: Heaven as Reunion

Heaven isn't just a place or time "out there," but the Communion of the Saints of all ages even in the here and now. It is a state of communion we actually experience, albeit fleetingly and at unexpected moments. This poem by Wendell Berry locates it at a country dance. Wherever it appears, it is a foretaste of the age to come.

The Wheel
WENDELL BERRY
for Robert Penn Warren

> At the first strokes of the fiddle bow
> the dancers rise from their seats.
> The dance begins to shape itself
> in the crowd, as couples join,
> and couples join couples, their movement
> together lightening their feet.
> They move in the ancient circle
> of the dance. The dance and the song
> call each other into being. Soon
> they are one—rapt in a single
> rapture, so that even the night
> has its clarity, and time
> is the wheel that brings it round.
>
> In this rapture the dead return.
> Sorrow is gone from them.
> They are light. They step
> into the steps of the living

and turn with them in the dance
in the sweet enclosure
of the song, and timeless
is the wheel that brings it round.

Drawn from Wendell Berry, *The Wheel* (San Francisco: North Point Press, 1982), 48.

Wednesday of the Fourth Week of Advent: A Cry for Renewal

In one way, this is not a very religious poem, nor did Judith Wright consider herself a religious poet. But it expresses our need to find meaning in the universe and in our lives, and it calls out to the lover we have missed for so long. Strangely, at the end, the speaker of the poem is not sure whether she has heard her own voice or another's—perhaps the voice of the seemingly long-absent beloved. The call to return works both ways.

Love Song in Absence
JUDITH WRIGHT

I sighed for a world left desolate without you,
all certainty, passion and peace withdrawn;
men like furious ants without the ant's humility,
their automatic days led in by mechanical dawn.

Voices all round me witnessed your unknown absence.
The stars clicked through their uncaring motions
because they imaged nothing. An unchecked cruelty
was born of winter and fear. Surgical lesions

hardened round hearts from which you had been removed.
Only museums remained. All difference was equated.
Columns of numbers and coins marched through the living flesh.
Relationship died away till all was separated.

You are gone, I said, and since through you I lived
I begin to die. Instruments have no song
except the living breath. You moved in the artery
that withers without blood. You are gone too long.

But as I sighed, I knew: incomprehensible energy
creates us and destroys, all words are made
in the long shadow of eternity.
Their meanings alter even as the thing is said.

And so, "Return," I cried, and at the word
was silent, wondering what voice I heard.

Drawn from Judith Wright, *Collected Poems 1942–1985* (Sydney: Angus & Robertson, 1994), 261.

Thursday of the Fourth Week of Advent: Heaven

The Incarnation of God the Word in the Infant of Bethlehem
sets in motion a sequence of events that leads to the Crucifixion and, beyond it, to the opening up of a new possibility for
human life, the heavenly life characterized by peace, love, and
constancy.

In this poem, Henry Vaughan paints a vision of a country
guarded by "beauteous files" of angels, under the command of
the one born in a manger, who risked all for love of human
beings.

Peace
HENRY VAUGHAN

> My Soul, there is a country,
> > Far beyond the stars,
> Where stands a wingéd sentry
> > All skillful in the wars.
> There above noise and danger
> > Sweet peace sits crown'd with smiles,
> And one born in a manger
> > Commands the beauteous files.
> He is thy gracious friend
> > And (O my Soul awake!)
> Did in pure love descend
> > To die here for thy sake.
> If thou canst get but thither,
> > There grows the flower of peace,
> The rose that cannot wither,
> > Thy fortress and thy ease.

Leave then thy foolish ranges;
    For none can thee secure,
But one who never changes,
    Thy God, thy life, thy cure.

Drawn from *Henry Vaughan: The Complete Poems*, edited by Alan Rudrum (New Haven: Yale University Press, 1981), 185–86.

Friday of the Fourth Week of Advent: Mary and the Child

Alice Meynell writes of Jesus here as child not only of Mary but also of the whole world of nature. The earth, in accordance with God's intention, feeds and clothes us.

The superscription is the Vulgate of Isaiah 45:8 and can be translated: "O heavens, send down your dew from above, and let the clouds rain down the Just One. Let the earth open and cause the Savior to spring up like a new plant." The verse was used in the Latin Mass on the First Sunday of Advent.

Advent Meditation

ALICE MEYNELL

> *Rorate coeli desuper, et nubes pluant Justum*
> *Aperiatur terra, et germinet Salvatorem.*

> No sudden thing of glory and fear
> Was the Lord's coming; but the dear
>   Slow Nature's days followed each other
>   To form the Savior from his Mother
> —One of the children of the year.

> The earth, the rain, received the trust,
> —The sun and dews, to frame the Just.
>   He drew His daily life from these,
>   According to His own decrees
> Who makes man from the fertile dust.

> Sweet summer and the winter wild,
> These brought him forth, the Undefiled.
>   The happy Springs renewed again
>   His daily bread, the growing grain,
> The food and raiment of the Child.

Drawn from *The Poems of Alice Meynell* (New York: Scribner, 1923), 37.

Christmas Eve

In this carol-like poem, Rossetti begins by playing with paradoxes: the darkness of Christmas is intensely light, its cold intensely warm. All this points to the paradoxical union of power and lowliness in the Infant of Bethlehem, the supreme love and power of the universe made approachable in this unexpected way. As often, Rossetti returns to bridal imagery to express the union of God and humanity in Christ.

Christmas Eve

CHRISTINA ROSSETTI

Christmas hath a darkness
Brighter than the blazing noon,
Christmas hath a chillness
Warmer than the heat of June,
Christmas hath a beauty
Lovelier than the world can show:
For Christmas bringeth Jesus,
Brought for us so low.

Earth, strike up your music,
 Birds that sing and bells that ring;
Heaven hath answering music
 For all Angels soon to sing:
Earth, put on your whitest
 Bridal robe of spotless snow:
For Christmas bringeth Jesus,
 Brought for us so low.

Drawn from *Christina Rossetti: The Complete Poems*, text by R. W. Crump (London: Penguin Books, 2001), 421–22.

Christmas Day

In this playful poem, George Herbert presents himself as a shepherd. His flock is made up of his own thoughts, which he feeds in the pasture of God's word and waters with God's grace. He offers this to explain why he, too, can join in the shepherds' Christmas music. Then he complains that the winter sun doesn't shine long or bright enough for their concert. He'll have to find a more reliable sun. Perhaps it is Jesus himself he hopes to find—"a willing shiner" who will never set and who will ultimately join us in the musical celebration of his own birth. At the last, one will no longer be able to distinguish between the light and the music.

There is a fine setting of this poem in Ralph Vaughan Williams's Christmas oratorio, *Hodie*.

Christmas

GEORGE HERBERT

> The shepherds sing; and shall I silent be?
>   My God, no hymn for Thee?
> My soul's a shepherd too: a flock it feeds
>   Of thoughts, and words, and deeds.

The pasture is Thy Word; the streams, Thy grace
    Enriching all the place.
Shepherd and flock shall sing, and all my powers
    Outsing the daylight hours.
Then we will chide the sun for letting night
    Take up his place and right:
We sing one common Lord; wherefore he should
    Himself the candle hold.
I will go searching, till I find a sun
    Shall stay till we have done—
A willing shiner, that shall shine as gladly
    As frost-nipped suns look sadly.
Then we will sing, and shine all our own day,
    And one another pay;
His beams shall cheer my breast, and both so twine
Till ev'n His beams sing, and my music shine.

Drawn from *The Works of George Herbert in Prose and Verse* (New York: Thomas Y. Crowell, n.d.), 167–68.

ST. STEPHEN'S DAY OR BOXING DAY

The Second Day of Christmas, December 26

We know the Feast of Stephen from John Mason Neal's popular carol "Good King Wencelas." It's also "Boxing Day" in Britain, variously explained as a day for exchanging presents or for taking food to the poor, just as in the carol.

In today's selection, we linger a moment over one of the essential moments of the new birth: Mary singing a lullaby to her baby. One gift evokes another. The infant evokes the lullaby. The gift of God's presence in the infant calls us to share our gifts with others. There is a beautiful setting of this text by Ralph Vaughan Williams, in his Christmas oratorio *Hodie*.

The Virgin's Lullaby

ANONYMOUS

> Sweet was the song the Virgin sang
> when she to Bethlem Judah came
> and was delivered of a son
> that blessed Jesus hath to name.
> Lulla, lulla, lulla, lullaby,
> lulla, lulla, lulla, lullaby.
>
> "Sweet babe," sang she,
> "my son and eke[1] a savior born,
> who hast vouchsaféd[2] from on high
> to visit us that were forlorn.
> Lalulla, lalulla, lalullaby,
> sweet babe," sang she,
> and rocked him sweetly on her knee.

---

1. "eke"—also

2. "vouchsafed"—consented

Drawn from *The Oxford Book of Carols*, edited by Percy Dearmer, R. Vaughan Williams, and Martin Shaw (London: Oxford University Press, 1928), 60–61. Its original source is the seventeenth-century manuscript *Lute Book* of William Ballet.

ST. JOHN'S DAY

The Third Day of Christmas, December 27

All but the last two lines of this poem are uttered by the angels, as they announce the new birth to the shepherds and send them scurrying off to see the baby Jesus. The angelic voices celebrate the paradox that meager human garments now swaddle the one whom the heavenly spheres cannot contain.

The Nativity

WILLIAM DRUMMOND

Run, shepherds, run where Bethlehem blest appears!
We bring the best of news. Be not dismay'd!
A Savior there is born, more old than years,
Amidst heav'n's rolling heights this earth who stay'd;[1]
In a poor cottage inn'd, a Virgin Maid
A weakling did him bear, who all upbears.[2]
This is he, poorly swaddled, in manger laid,
To whom too narrow swaddlings are our spheres.[3]
Run, shepherds, run, and solemnize his birth!
This is that Night—no, Day—grown great with bliss,
In which the power of Satan broken is.
In heaven be glory, peace unto the earth.
  Thus singing through the air the angels swam,
  And cope[4] of stars re-echoéd the same.

---

1. who steadied the earth in the midst of the universe

2. In poor lodgings, Mary bore, as a weak child, the one who bears up all worlds.

3. Even the heavenly spheres are too small to swaddle the divine Son.

4. "cope"—cloak, canopy

Drawn from *The Oxford Book of Seventeenth Century Verse*, chosen by H. J. C. Grierson and G. Bullough (Oxford: Clarendon Press, 1934) 264.

FEAST OF THE HOLY INNOCENTS
The Fourth Day of Christmas, December 28

This feast day commemorates the children of Bethlehem who were killed on the orders of King Herod (Matthew 2:16–18). We observe it here with a "wassail"—the kind of Christmas carol sung by wandering groups seeking hospitality from house-holders.

Hospitality, the virtue opposite to all violence, is basic to the celebration of Christmas. The old practice of wassailing gave people an opportunity to provide hospitality to friends, neighbors, and strangers—perhaps especially toward children. When we receive others as guests, we are reenacting the hospitality we wish had been extended to Joseph and Mary.

This carol is a modern variation of the old wassail songs. It appears in the Christmas chapter of Kenneth Grahame's *The Wind in the Willows*, where it is sung by the field-mice children. Appropriately, it celebrates the particular privilege of the animals in the stable who were "the first to cry Nowell."

The field mice get the Christmas story a little confused here, but to good purpose. The star that guides the Magi in Matthew's Gospel has here become a guide to Joseph and Mary and even to the carolers themselves.

Carol
KENNETH GRAHAME

> Villagers all, this frosty tide,
> Let your doors swing open wide,
> Though wind may follow, and snow beside,
> Yet draw us in by your fire to bide;
>   Joy shall be yours in the morning!

Here we stand in the cold and the sleet,
Blowing fingers and stamping feet,
Come from far away you to greet—
You by the fire and we in the street—
    Bidding you joy in the morning!

For ere one half of the night was gone,
Sudden a star has led us on,
Raining bliss and benison—
Bliss tomorrow and more anon,
    Joy for every morning!

Goodman Joseph toiled through the snow—
Saw the star o'er a stable low;
Mary she might not further go—
Welcome thatch, and litter below!
    Joy was hers in the morning!

And then they heard the angels tell
"Who were the first to cry Nowell?
Animals all, as it befell,
In the stable where they did dwell!
    Joy shall be theirs in the morning!"

Drawn from Kenneth Grahame, *The Wind in the Willows* (New York: The Heritage Press, 1944), 72.

The Fifth Day of Christmas, December 29

Many know Christina Rossetti's Christmas carols, "In the bleak midwinter" and "Love came down at Christmas." In this carol, she focuses on those who observed Jesus' birth in the cold stable, a very odd mixture of ox and ass, saint and angel. We watch and rejoice with them, even while most of the world, including the people of great power, sleep and know nothing of the great change God has just wrought.

A Christmas Carol

CHRISTINA ROSSETTI

> Before the paling of the stars
>   Before the winter morn
> Before the earliest cockcrow
>   Jesus Christ was born:
> Born in a stable
>   Cradled in a manger,
> In the world His Hands had made
>   Born a Stranger.
>
> Priest and King lay fast asleep
>   In Jerusalem,
> Young and Old lay fast asleep
>   In crowded Bethlehem:
> Saint and Angel Ox and Ass
>   Kept a watch together
> Before the Christmas daybreak
>   In the winter weather.

Jesus on His Mother's breast
  In the stable cold,
Spotless Lamb of God was He,
  Shepherd of the Fold:
Let us kneel with Mary Maid
  With Joseph bent and hoary
With Saint and Angel Ox and Ass
  To hail the King of Glory.

Drawn from *Christina Rossetti: The Complete Poems*, text by R. W. Crump (London: Penguin Books, 2001), 564–65.

The Sixth Day of Christmas, December 30

The shepherds must have been quite bewildered to find their tedious, cold night's work disrupted by a crowd of resplendent angels, singing music finer than they had ever heard and hurrying them off to Bethlehem to see something they could never have imagined. We have a trip to make, too, if we want to see the infant—a trip we make within our own lives, the trip from certainty to bewilderment to the astonishing recognition of God's presence already here, already open to us.

Going to God with the Shepherds
LOUIS WILLIAM COUNTRYMAN

> If you want to go to God, go without
> your certainties. Take your graces. Leave
> your certainties behind. If you go looking
> for a Triangle inside a Trefoil[1] inside
> a Conundrum, you'll miss the greatest sight
> of all, the Holy Trinity playing
> children's games on the lawns of heaven. If
> you only look for the Virgin of the Window,[2]
> you'll walk right past Our Lady, laughing and telling
> stories with a group of friends.
> > The disciples

---

1. Triangle and trefoil are symbols of the doctrine of the Trinity, which is itself always a mystery or conundrum.

2. The Virgin of the Window is the great stained-glass portrayal of Mary in the Cathedral of Chartres; but any great portrait of her would serve the purpose of the poem.

knew not the Lord Jesus in his resurrection
flesh. They were expecting someone else,
someone they knew for certain. And this was like,
but was it he? They knew him only when
he handed them their bread.[3]

         Go to God, then,
taking in the hand of memory
the silken light of a clear dawn after
wet weather and say, with tears if need be,
"You made this." Take the name of your beloved
and say, "You made him and in him you remade me."
Take the goodness of your life. And take
some moment of uncertain and life-giving
hope, like an angel whispering or—sometimes—
trumpeting in your ear. These are your guides.

         And so
go with the shepherds on their angelic quest.
Go to that hick town that David left
as soon as he got the chance, go to the stable,
see what you never expected to see, the doors
to God opening in that manger against
all certainty.

         And then return to find
anew the tracks of grace: the beauty of men,
the beauty of women, the delight of children,
the running of a swift dog, the flight of birds,
the sweetness of a pear, hands held in quiet.
If you want to go to God, leave your certainties
behind. But be sure to take your graces.

---

3. Luke 24:13–31.

NEW YEAR'S EVE
The Seventh Day of Christmas, December 31

This is the poem that gave us the classic line for New Year's Eve: "Ring out the old, ring in the new." By itself, it is in danger of seeming trite because it is too familiar. In the larger context of "In Memoriam," with its unflinching exploration of grief, it has quite a different quality. It captures the soul of the bereaved person, rising at last from prolonged mourning to recognize that the very love that made the lost beloved so important to us calls us to pay attention again to the world around us and to hope and work for a better future.

The image of "the Christ that is to be" echoes the Advent theme of the Second Coming, but also suggests that we may have a part to play in helping all people find a way to live as citizens of the age to come, by creating here and now a world of peace and justice.

In Memoriam, CVI
ALFRED TENNYSON

> Ring out, wild bells, to the wild sky,
> The flying cloud, the frosty light:
> The year is dying in the night;
> Ring out, wild bells, and let him die.
>
> Ring out the old, ring in the new,
> Ring, happy bells, across the snow
> The year is going, let him go;
> Ring out the false, ring in the true.

Ring out the grief that saps the mind,
 For those that here we see no more;
 Ring out the feud of rich and poor,
Ring in redress to all mankind.

Ring out a slowly dying cause,
 And ancient forms of party strife;
 Ring in the nobler modes of life,
With sweeter manners, purer laws.

Ring out the want, the care, the sin,
 The faithless coldness of the times;
 Ring out, ring out my mournful rhymes,
But ring the fuller minstrel in.

Ring out false pride in place and blood,
 The civic slander and the spite;
 Ring in the love of truth and right,
Ring in the common love of good.

Ring out old shapes of foul disease;
 Ring out the narrowing lust of gold
 Ring out the thousand wars of old,
Ring in the thousand years of peace.

Ring in the valiant man and free,
 The larger heart, the kindlier hand.
 Ring out the darkness of the land,
Ring in the Christ that is to be.

Drawn from Alfred Tennyson, *In Memoriam* (Chicago: Henneberry, n.d.),
94–95.

FEAST OF THE HOLY NAME OF JESUS
OR NEW YEAR'S DAY

The Eighth Day of Christmas, January 1

According to Luke 2:21, the infant Jesus was circumcised and named on the eighth day after birth, as Torah requires. New Year's Day has many other associations for people now, but it has a long history as the Feast of the Circumcision, now more commonly called the Feast of the Holy Name.

In today's poem, George Herbert plays a game with the name "Jesus," giving it a kind of etymological "explanation" in English. He was helped by the fact that in older versions of our alphabet, there was no letter "J," only "I." Accordingly, he was equally free to spell the name "Iesu."

JESU

GEORGE HERBERT

> JESU is in my heart, His sacred name
> Is deeply carved there: but the other week
> A great affliction broke the little frame
> E'en all to pieces, which I went to seek:
> And first I found the corner where was J,
> After where ES, and next where U was graved.
> When I had got these parcels, instantly
> I sat me down to spell them, and perceived
> That to my broken heart He was "I ease you,"
> And to my whole is JESU.

Drawn from *The Works of George Herbert in Prose and Verse* (New York: Thomas Y. Crowell, n.d.), 204.

The Ninth Day of Christmas, January 2

This delightful poem, found in a late-seventeenth-century manuscript, is a Christmas "pastoral" or shepherds' song. The poet disclaims all need for fancy music, though he creates some as he goes! He tells his heart to tighten its strings, like a lute, to match the angels' pitch, even if it risks breaking. And we share our song not only with the angelic chorus, but with the lowly animals in the shed as well.

On Christmas Day to My Heart

CLEMENT PAMAN

Today,
Hark! Heaven sings!
Stretch, tune my Heart
(For hearts have strings
May bear their part)
And though thy lute were bruis'd i'th' fall,[1]
Bruis'd hearts may reach an humble pastoral.[2]

Today
Shepherds rejoice—
And angels do
No more. Thy voice
Can reach that, too.
Bring then at least thy pipe along[3]
And mingle consort with the angels' song.

---

1. The human heart was damaged in the Fall (Genesis 3), like a stringed instrument being dropped.

2. Even a damaged instrument is good enough for folk music!

3. The heart is compared to a stringed instrument and the voice to a wind instrument.

Today
A shed that's thatch'd
(Yet straws can sing)[4]
Holds God; God's match'd
With beasts. Beasts bring
Their song their way; for shame, then, raise
Thy notes. Lambs bleat and oxen bellow praise.

Today
God honor'd Man
Not angels; yet
They sing. And can
Rais'd man forget?[5]
Praise is our debt today, nor shall
Angels (man's not so poor) discharge it all.

Today,
Then, screw thee high,
My Heart—up to
The angels' key.
Sing Glory, do!
What if thy strings all crack and fly?
On such a ground, musick 'twill be to die.

Drawn from *The Oxford Book of Seventeenth Century Verse*, chosen by H. J. C. Grierson and G. Bullough (Oxford: Clarendon Press, 1934), 825–26.

---

4. Shepherds' pipes were made of dried reeds.

5. The dignity of humanity was raised, by the Incarnation, above that of the angels; cf. Hebrews 2:5-18.

The Tenth Day of Christmas, January 3

Christmastide, in the northern hemisphere, often has strong associations with the winter solstice—the darkest, coldest time of year. But in the southern hemisphere, the weather is likely to be the exact opposite. We have two poems today, one for a winter Christmas, one for a summer one.

The first poem, by Christina Rossetti, has become well known, in its beautiful setting by Gustav Holst, as a Christmas carol. Unfortunately, some collections omit the wonderful third verse.

The second poem, by New Zealand poet and composer Colin Gibson, brings to life a hot-weather Christmas. As Gibson writes, "The Folly of Love takes off from St. Paul on the foolishness of God, marvelously mirrored I think in our frantic behavior at Christmas."

A Christmas Carol
CHRISTINA ROSSETTI

> In the bleak mid-winter
> Frosty wind made moan,
> Earth stood hard as iron,
> Water like a stone;
> Snow had fallen, snow on snow,
> Snow on snow,
> In the bleak mid-winter
> Long ago.
>
> Our God, Heaven cannot hold Him
> Nor earth sustain;
> Heaven and earth shall flee away
> When He comes to reign:

In the bleak mid-winter
    A stable-place sufficed
The Lord God Almighty
    Jesus Christ.

Enough for Him whom cherubim
    Worship night and day,
A breastful of milk
    And a mangerful of hay;
Enough for Him whom angels
    Fall down before,
The ox and ass and camel
    Which adore.

Angels and archangels
    May have gathered there,
Cherubim and seraphim
    Throng'd the air,
But only His mother
    In her maiden bliss
Worshipped the Beloved
    With a kiss.

What can I give Him,
    Poor as I am?
If I were a shepherd
    I would bring a lamb,
If I were a wise man
    I would do my part—
Yet what I can I give Him,
    Give my heart.

Drawn from *Christina Rossetti: The Complete Poems*, text by R. W. Crump (London: Penguin Books, 2001), 210–11.

COLIN GIBSON

There's straw in the manger and babies in danger,
some shepherds possessed by the folly of love.[1]
The register's ringing, the shop choirs are singing,
it's bargains galore in the folly of love.
It's midsummer madness and everyday badness;
the usual scene for the coming of Christ.
It's parcels and wrapping, it's father caught napping,
and children awake in the folly of love.

It's suntan and lotion, it's surf and commotion,
it's sand in the sandwiches, folly of love.
It's crackers and candles, it's shorts and it's sandals,
plum pudding in summer, the folly of love.
It's friends and relations, it's neighbors and nations
enjoying a moment of peace and goodwill.
It's crowds at the local, old aunties gone vocal,
and "house full" signs out, O the folly of love.

It's families united, it's grandmas delighted,
it's long-distance calls in the folly of love.
It's caravans, camels and fellows in flannels,
three kings chasing stars for the folly of love.
It's postcard Madonnas receiving full honors,
Saint Nicholas wearing a cotton wool beard.
It's trees hung with baubles, angelical warbles,
and God come to earth in the folly of love.

By permission of the author.

---

1. Cf. 1 Corinthians 1:18–31, where Paul writes that God's foolishness is
stronger than human wisdom.

The Eleventh Day of Christmas, January 4

John Keble not only celebrates the music of the angels, but also pinpoints the exact moment when they began to sing—not, he observes, at the grand announcement of David's royal heir, but at the humble words about the manger, given to the shepherds as a sign by which they would recognize the child. Even in our own time, Keble says, the child Jesus becomes known to those who seek him in quiet and humility.

Christmas Day

JOHN KEBLE

And suddenly there was with the Angel a multitude of the heavenly host praising God. *St. Luke* ii. 13.

> What sudden blaze of song,
>   Spreads o'er th'expanse of Heav'n?
> In waves of light it thrills along,
>   Th'angelic signal given—
> "Glory to God!" from yonder central fire
> Flows out the echoing lay[1] beyond the starry choir;
>
> Like circles widening round
>   Upon a clear blue river,
> Orb after orb, the wondrous sound
>   Is echoed on for ever:
> "Glory to God on high, on earth be peace,
> And love towards men of love—salvation and release."

---

1. "lay"—medieval term for "song"

Yet stay,[2] before thou dare
    To join that festal throng;
Listen and mark what gentle air
    First stirr'd the tide of song;
'Tis not, "the Savior born in David's home,
To whom for power and health obedient worlds
                should come"—

'Tis not, "the Christ the Lord"—
    With fix'd adoring look
The choir of Angels caught the word,
    Nor yet their silence broke.
But when they heard the sign where Christ should be,
In sudden light they shone and heavenly harmony.

Wrapp'd in His swaddling bands,
    And in His manger laid,
The Hope and Glory of all lands
    Is come to the world's aid:
No peaceful home upon His cradle smil'd,
Guests rudely went and came, where slept the royal Child.

But where Thou dwellest, Lord,
    No other thought should be.
Once duly welcom'd and ador'd,
    How should I part with Thee?
Bethlehem must lose Thee soon, but Thou wilt grace
The single heart to be Thy sure abiding-place.

Thee, on the bosom laid
    Of a pure virgin mind,
In quiet ever and in shade,
    Shepherd and sage may find;
They who have bow'd untaught to Nature's sway,
And they who follow Truth along her star-pav'd way.

---

2. "stay"—wait

The pastoral spirits first
　　Approach Thee, Babe divine,
For they in lowly thoughts are nurs'd,
　　Meet for Thy lowly shrine:
Sooner than they should miss where Thou dost dwell,
Angels from Heaven will stoop to guide them to Thy cell.

　　Still, as the day comes round
　　　For Thee to be reveal'd,
By wakeful shepherds Thou art found,
　　　Abiding in the field.
All through the wintry heaven and chill night air,
In music and in light Thou dawnest on their prayer.

　　O faint not ye for fear—
　　　What though your wandering sheep,
Reckless of what they see and hear,
　　　Lie lost in willful sleep?
High Heaven in mercy to your sad annoy[3]
Still greets you with glad tidings of immortal joy.

　　Think on th' eternal home
　　　The Savior left for you;
Think on the Lord most holy, come
　　　To dwell with hearts untrue:
So shall ye tread untir'd His pastoral ways,
And in the darkness sing your carol of high praise.

Drawn from John Keble, *The Christian Year: Thoughts in Verse for the Sundays and Holydays throughout the Year* (New York: James Miller, 1879), 33-36.

---

3. "annoy"—annoyance, distress

The Twelfth Day of Christmas, January 5

The evening of this day is Twelfthnight, the end of the Christmas season and the prelude to the season of Epiphany or "revelation," which celebrates the moments when we become newly aware of God at work in our world, meeting us even in the midst of our everyday lives.

The Twelfth Day is traditionally the time to clear out the evergreens brought indoors to decorate for Christmas. The speaker of this poem, working through this chore and momentarily blinded by the low winter sun, rediscovers the grace of Incarnation—God's daring to become one of us in the Baby of Bethlehem—and the hope of epiphany.

A Silent Promise
JAY EMERSON JOHNSON

> Light comes back
> as it always does
> just before Christmas Day
> like finding a treasured keepsake
> forgotten in attic recesses
> and I start to think about Hoovering up
> brittle evergreen needles,
> fingering the stubborn ones
> out from a wooly carpet's fibers.

Light comes back slowly
tracing an ancient arc
across the winter sky
and I kneel on hardwood
straining to scoop up
a stray ornament
from a dusty corner
just out of reach
with sunlight
dappling my vision.

Light comes back
with a promise
silent as the stars—
this simple, tender flesh
covering our hands
wrinkling our knees
layering our faces
shall be seen
revealed as a divine gift
    for this world
indeed, an epiphany.

The Feast of the Epiphany,
January 6

Sidney Godolphin holds up the shepherds' love alongside the wisdom of the Magi to say that love is the true crown of wisdom. The wise try to "ascend to nature's highest cause" and seek "the cause of causes, end of ends"—all ultimately to be found in God. But their wisdom reaches its goal and achieves its purpose in wonder and love, things equally available to the simplest shepherd. Both groups attend on the birth of Jesus, uniting knowledge and love in the contemplation of this supreme object.

SIDNEY GODOLPHIN

> Lord, when the wise men came from far,
> Led to thy cradle by a star,
> Then did the shepherds, too, rejoice,
> Instructed by thy Angel's voice.
> Blest were the wise men in their skill,
> And shepherds in their harmless will.
>
> Wise men, in tracing nature's laws,
> Ascend unto the highest cause;
> Shepherds with humble fearfulness

Walk safely, though their light be less:
Though wise men better know the way,
It seems no honest heart can stray.

There is no merit in the wise
But love—the shepherds' sacrifice.
Wise men, all ways of knowledge past,
To th' shepherds' wonder come at last;
To know can only wonder breed,
And not to know is wonder's seed.

A wise man at the altar bows
And offers up his studied vows
And is received. May not the tears
Which spring too from a shepherd's fears
And sighs upon his frailty spent,
Though not distinct, be eloquent?

'Tis true, the object sanctifies
All passions[1] which within us rise,
But since no creature comprehends
The cause of causes, end of ends,
He who himself vouchsafes to know[2]
Best pleases his creator so.

When then our sorrows we apply
To our own wants and poverty,
When we look up in all distress
And our own misery confess,
Sending both thanks and prayers above,
Then though we do not know, we love.

Drawn from *The Oxford Book of Seventeenth Century Verse*, chosen by H. J. C.
Grierson and G. Bullough (Oxford: Clarendon Press, 1934), 572–73.

---

1. Our desires are only as good as their objects.

2. the person who takes the trouble to gain self-knowledge

The Poets

Wendell Berry (1934–)

Wendell Berry, poet, novelist, and essayist, works the land his family has farmed for generations in Kentucky. He speaks out for the land and for the kind of immediate connection with it that he feels can sustain a better human life than our technology-oriented modern culture affords.

L. William Countryman (1941–)

Born in Oklahoma City, Louis William Countryman became an Episcopalian in his teen years and was ordained a priest in his twenties. He has served parishes and taught New Testament, Greek, and spirituality. Besides being editor of this collection, he is an occasional poet.

Bruce Dawe (1930–)

One of Australia's most popular poets, Bruce Dawe writes in an idiom that is both complex and accessible. He has served in the Australian Air Force as well as being a writer and teacher. The topics of his poetry range from personal experience to the world of nature to public events. Some are in colloquial Australian voices, including his powerful account of the Crucifixion from the perspective of the centurion in command, "And a Good Friday Was Had by All."

Emily Dickinson (1830–86)

Emily Elizabeth Dickinson lived most of her life in the town of Amherst, Massachusetts. Though she has the reputation of a recluse, she was in fact well aware of currents of thought in the larger world. When she was in school at Mount Holyoke Female Seminary, she resisted the pressure to profess Christianity in the current revivalist fashion. But the older, more inward Calvinism of New England seems to have retained an influence on her. Many of her poems are in the hymn meters used by Isaac Watts. She published almost nothing during her lifetime. Like Gerald Manley Hopkins, her use of language and poetic form was advanced for her time and probably seemed difficult to many in her limited circle of readers. Christina Rossetti lived to read and admire the first published volume of her poetry.

Philip Doddridge (1702–51)

Philip Doddridge was a "Dissenter," that is an English Protestant who refused to be part of the Church of England. He was ordained as a presbyter and was an energetic preacher, teacher, and pastor. He promoted unity among Protestants of all kinds, even attempting to organize exchange of pulpits with Church of England clergy. He followed the example of his older friend, Isaac Watts, in writing hymns, a number of which are still in wide use (e.g., "O God of Bethel" and "My God, thy table now is spread").

John Donne (1571/2–1631)

John Donne was born to a Roman Catholic family, but became a member of the Church of England in his twenties. He was highly esteemed as a poet in his own day and, after a period of eclipse in the eighteenth and nineteenth centuries, is again regarded as one of the greatest poets of the English language. His love poetry got him a reputation as a rake. And he destroyed his hopes for advancement in government by eloping with the daughter of his patron. It was only reluctantly and at the express desire of King James I that he consented to be ordained. He was made Dean of St. Paul's Cathedral in London in 1621. His sacred poems show a strong consciousness of sin. His balancing consciousness of grace is perhaps better revealed in his many sermons and his famous *Devotions upon Emergent Occasions*, prompted by a near-fatal illness.

William Drummond (1585–1649)

The Scottish poet William Drummond succeeded his father as laird of Hawthornden and lived a relatively retired life there. He was unusual at the time among Scottish poets in deciding to write in English, perhaps because he wrote at a time when James VI of Scotland had succeeded Elizabeth I as King of England and was bringing the two realms together. He lived through turbulent times under James's son Charles I and in the period of the Civil War, both of which brought profound religious disturbances to Scotland.

Colin Gibson (1933–)

Colin Gibson describes himself as "a New Zealander by birth and native loyalty." He is Professor Emeritus at the University of Otago, Dunedin, New Zealand, where he has taught English literature and drama for over forty years. He is church organist and choirmaster at the Mornington Methodist Church, Dunedin, and has been writing hymns (both musical settings and texts) and composing other religious and secular music, much of it choral, since about 1960. He is a founding member of the editorial team of *The New Zealand Hymnbook*.

Sidney Godolphin (1610–43)

Under King Charles I, Sidney Godolphin was active in politics as a Member of Parliament. He died fighting on the royalist side in the Civil War. Much of his poetry remained unpublished until the early twentieth century.

Kenneth Grahame (1859–1931)

Born in Scotland and orphaned early in life, Grahame was raised by relatives in England. As an adult, he worked in the Bank of England, but devoted himself to writing about childhood and for children. *The Wind in the Willows* is an animal fable of epic quality, beloved by generations of readers, old and young. Though not primarily a poet, Grahame edited the *Cambridge Book of Poetry for Young People*.

Kevin Hart (1954–)

Kevin Hart is one of Australia's major contemporary poets. He teaches at Monash University and is known for his prose writing as well as his poetry. He edited *The Oxford Book of Australian Religious Verse*.

George Herbert (1593–1633)

A younger contemporary of John Donne, George Herbert also aimed at a career in government but was persuaded to accept ordination as a priest in the Church of England in 1630. He lived out the few years remaining to him as the parish priest of Bemerton, near (now really in) the cathedral town of Salisbury. He entrusted his remarkable collection of poems, *The Temple*, to his friend Nicholas Ferrar, who published it after his death. Unlike the work of many of his contemporaries, Herbert's poetry has never ceased to be read and admired by succeeding generations.

Robert Herrick (1591–1674)

One of the poets known as "sons of Ben [Jonson]," Robert Herrick is best known for his light, elegant, witty poems about beauty and love. But he was also a priest in the Church of England and ministered to a parish in Devon from 1629. He was deprived of that post from 1645 to 1660 because of his royalist politics and his Anglican religion, but he lived long enough to return to it after the monarchy and the Book of Common Prayer were restored in the early 1660s. His religious poems, while more sober than his secular ones, show the same delight in grace (in all senses of the word) and a sense that God is a great deal friendlier than his Puritan opponents were prepared to allow.

Gerald Manley Hopkins (1844–89)

Son of a Church of England family, Gerald Manley Hopkins became a Roman Catholic while at university and subsequently became a Jesuit and a priest. He was a highly educated and philosophically profound thinker and also a highly original poet—too much so, it seems, for his own time. He had the encouragement of a few major contemporary poets, including Robert Bridges, who began publishing his poetry after his death. It was decades, though, before he came to be recognized as a major figure of English literature.

Jay Emerson Johnson (1961–)

Raised in a conservative Evangelical context, Jay Johnson became an Episcopalian while in college and is a priest in the Episcopal Church. He has served parishes in Chicago and the San Francisco Bay Area. He is also a scholar in the field of theology and the author of *Dancing with God: Anglican Christianity and the Practice of Hope*. He has the custom of writing an Advent/Christmas greeting to his friends in poetic genre, one of which appears in this collection.

John Keble (1792–1866)

Son of a priest in the Church of England, John Keble was himself ordained priest in 1816. An admirer of William Wordsworth, he published his own collection of poems, *The Christian Year*, in 1827 and not long after was elected professor of poetry at Oxford. He combined academic brilliance with devotion to the catholic traditions of the Church of England. In 1833, he preached a sermon generally considered the beginning of the Oxford Movement, which set about reemphasizing that heritage. He endured much hostility as a result but remained a leader of the movement and a devoted parish priest throughout his life.

Alice Meynell (1847–1922)

An Englishwoman, Alice Christiana Gertrude Thompson converted to Roman Catholicism in her twenties. She subsequently married Wilfred Meynell. Her small body of poetry, composed over many years, combines strong devotion with deep reflection.

Clement Paman (1612–63)

Like Herrick, Clement Paman was an Anglican priest and a royalist who lived through the period of Puritan domination under the Commonwealth. Since the Puritans forbade the observance of Christmas, the celebration of it in the poem presented here may be seen partly as an act of resistance. He lost his clerical position during the Commonwealth, but, after the restoration of the monarchy in 1660, became Dean of Elphin in Ireland. His poetry survived primarily in manuscript form.

Christina Rossetti (1830–94)

Christina Georgina Rossetti lived a quiet, retired life in a culturally exciting environment. One of her brothers was Dante Gabriel Rossetti, painter, poet, and leader of the Pre-Raphaelite

Brotherhood. (The young Christina sat as model for a number of early paintings.) The family was of Italian origin, but had come to England because of her grandfather's resistance to papal government in Italy. While Christina was devoted to the emerging Anglo-Catholic movement in the nineteenth-century Church of England (her sister joined one of the first religious orders for women), she remained staunchly anti-papal. Her own health deteriorated badly in adulthood, and she remained at home caring for her mother until the latter's death. During this time, she achieved very high esteem as a poet. At the death of Tennyson, some proposed her to succeed him as Poet Laureate; but the idea of a woman in this post was apparently too daring for the time. Her reputation as a poet, like that of many of her Victorian contemporaries, suffered an eclipse in the mid-twentieth century. But as her work re-emerges into wider availability, it is becoming apparent how rich and accomplished it is.

Elizabeth J. Smith (1956–)

A priest in the Anglican Church of Australia, Elizabeth Smith is a parish pastor in Melbourne. She is also a scholar of liturgy and a writer of hymns that embody deep Christian faith in a distinctly contemporary idiom. She seeks not just to avoid language that strikes the modern ear as less than inclusive, but actively to retrieve and celebrate other elements of the Christian liturgical tradition that have been ignored and underutilized in the past. The result is a body of hymns that seem both familiar and new.

Alfred Tennyson (1809–92)

Esteemed by critics and the public alike, Alfred Tennyson was widely considered the greatest English poet of his own day and was long the British Poet Laureate. The son of a priest in the Church of England, he was able to give voice to the doubts of the nineteenth century and yet remain connected with the church, being a friend and supporter of the theologian F. D. Maurice. "In Memoriam," with its frank account of his grief over the death of his friend Arthur Henry Hallam, is a key work of Victorian spirituality. Like the other Victorian poets, his reputation faded after his death, but he is again recognized as one of the great poets of the English language.

R. S. Thomas (1913–2000)

Ronald Stuart Thomas was a priest in the (Anglican) Church in Wales. His poetry captured the Welsh countryside, the challenges of life there, and the spiritual struggle of seeking God in a century when that undertaking was far from easy. A wide readership found spiritual nurture in them, perhaps partly because they also dash cold water in the face of any sort of religious sentimentality. Though of Welsh origins, he learned the Welsh language only in his thirties. He wrote poetry in his first language, English, but came to use Welsh for his extensive writing in prose.

Henry Vaughan (1622–95)

Born in Wales of a Welsh family and probably bilingual, Henry Vaughan wrote his poetry primarily in English. He was a layman and a physician but well educated in matters of theology, perhaps partly through having a brother who was a priest in the Church of England. Much of Vaughan's poetry was written during the Commonwealth, when the Book of Common Prayer and other aspects of Anglican observance (e.g., Christmas) were suppressed; and he was very hostile to the then-dominant Puritanism. But his great model was George Herbert, and Herbert's example helped prevent polemics from taking central place in Vaughan's poetry. Like Herbert, he is one of the great masters of English verse.

Judith Wright (1915–2000)

Born to a family of farmers and ranchers in New South Wales, Judith Wright grew up with a strong awareness of place and history. She was educated in Anglican schools and, though she did not find the spiritual depth she sought there and never defined herself in relation to any organized religion, she was shaped by that tradition in ways more profound than she may consciously have recognized. She wrote not only poetry but fiction, including a novel based on the story of her family. Her poetry is concerned both with personal experience and with the great world issues of the twentieth century. She became a strong champion of the environment and of the rights of aboriginal peoples in Australia.

William Butler Yeats (1865–1939)

Yeats is esteemed as a foremost poet of the twentieth century. He was a central figure in the Irish Literary Renaissance, both as a lyric poet and also as a playwright and a founder of the Irish National Theatre (commonly known as Abbey Theatre) in Dublin. He was a great admirer of William Blake and was influenced by Celtic folklore and mythology and by occult ideas.

ACKNOWLEDGMENTS

When my friend and editor Debra Farrington suggested this project to me, I resisted at first because of other obligations. In the event, however, the work of reading, reflection, and selection of the poems proved a welcome refreshment of the spirit in the midst of more mundane tasks. I could not know at the time that, in the final days of work on it, it would also fill a healing role as I experienced the deaths of a dear friend, of my brother, and of two beloved associates in work and faith.

My thanks to Elizabeth Smith for introducing me to Colin Gibson and to his delightful carol and to Jay Johnson for permission to use what began as a private communication.

My thanks to the Trustees of the Church Divinity School of the Pacific for the sabbatical leave during which parts of this work were done.

My thanks to Debra and other associates at Morehouse Publishing who furthered this work with their labors in securing permissions for poems under copyright and finding the cover art.

A Blessed Christmas to them and to all the readers of this book!

INDEX OF POETS

PERMISSIONS